THE
WHATCHAMACALLIT
BOOK

by Bernice Kohn Hunt

pictures by Tomie de Paola

G.P. Putnam's Sons · New York

FOR ELIZABETH AND EMILY

Text copyright ©1976 by Bernice Kohn Hunt
Illustrations copyright ©1976 by Tomie de Paola
All rights reserved. Published simultaneously in
Canada by Longman Canada Limited, Toronto.

Library of Congress Cataloging in Publication Data
Hunt, Bernice Kohn. The whatchamacallit book.
SUMMARY: Under such section headings as "Gizmos You
Might See around the House" and "Whatchamacallits
You Might See on a Trip" the reader is invited to name
the elusive words for dozens of definitions such as
"the feelers of insects," "the roller in a typewriter,"
and "a boat race."
1. Vocabulary—Juvenile literature. [I. Vocabulary]
I. De Paola, Thomas Anthony. II. Title.
PE1449.H85 428'.1 76-18831
ISBN 0-399-20521-7 ISBN 0-399-61011-1 lib. bdg.
Printed in the United States of America

Do you know the name of that thingamajig that holds up a lampshade? Or the whosit with diamonds in it that a queen wears on her head when she goes to a party? Or the whatchamacallit a doctor wraps around your arm to take your blood pressure?

The world is full of thingamajigs, whosits, and whatchamacallits—familiar objects or persons whose names you don't know or can't remember. How many of the following can *you* name?

DOOJIGGERS YOU MIGHT BE WEARING NOW

1. The opening, containing a zipper or other fastening device, that enables you to get into or out of blue jeans.

2. A decoration made of the same or a different fabric attached to a cloth object.

3. The hole in a shoe or a sneaker that you put the shoelace through.

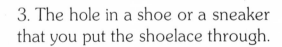

1. placket
2. appliqué
3. eyelet

4. temple 5. crown 6. toe cap

4. The sidepiece on a pair of eyeglasses, the part that fits over the ear.

5. The little knob you turn to wind your watch.

6. A piece of leather or other material that covers the toe of a shoe.

7. A jeweled coronet that a woman wears on her head.

8. A mask that covers half the face.

9. The metal rim that holds a gem in place on a piece of jewelry.

10. A fancy fastening on the front of a coat consisting of a button and a loop.

TAXI

GIZMOS YOU MIGHT SEE AROUND THE HOUSE

1. A stand with hooks for holding hats or coats.

2. The part behind a step that you bump your toes against.

3. The part of a step that you step on.

4. The handle of a bucket.

1. hall tree
(also, hat tree,
clothes tree)
2. riser
3. tread
4. bail

5. A transom window having the shape of a semicircle.

6. The overhead piece across the top of a doorway or window.

7. The side of a doorway or window opening.

8. The raised piece of flooring across the bottom of a doorway.

9. The little part that screws on top
of a lampshade to keep it in place.

9.

10. The kind of wall switch that
is commonly used to turn lights
on and off.

10.

11.

11. The metal frame that holds
a lampshade over a bulb.

12. The outlet in the wall that
you stick electric plugs into.

12.

13. A piece of furniture with shelves for bric-a-brac.

14. A doily for the backs or armrests of chairs.

15. A strip of material, cord, or the like used to hold a curtain to one side.

16. The part of a telephone you listen to.

17. The part of the telephone you speak into.

18. A small wheel on the end of a furniture leg.

19. The piano pedal on the right, often called, incorrectly, the loud pedal.

20. A thick, firm cushion used as a footstool or for kneeling.

21. A glass bottle used for serving oil or vinegar.

21.

22. A cooked mixture of corn kernels and beans.

22.

23. A large covered dish used for serving soup.

23.

24. tine
25. skewer
26. slice
27. trap

24. The prong of a fork.

25. A long pin of wood or metal that is used to hold meat or poultry together during cooking.

26. A knife with a broad flat blade used for cutting and serving.

27. The curved pipe underneath a sink drain.

28. The dimple in the bottom of an apple.

29. Strong brown paper used for bags or wrapping.

29.

30. A blanket or coverlet made of crocheted squares.

30.

28. basin
29. kraft
30. afghan

31. A sheet of paper folded to form two leaves, one of which is pasted flat to the inside cover of a book, the other forming a flyleaf.

32. The roller in a typewriter.

33. A decorative metal plate around a keyhole, doorknob, drawer pull, etc.

34. The free-swinging bracket of a record player that holds the pickup.

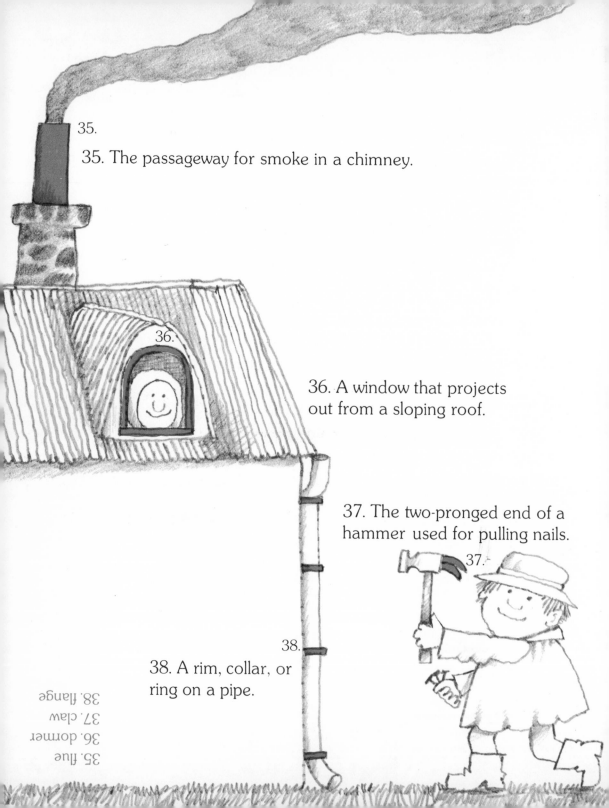

35.

35. The passageway for smoke in a chimney.

36. A window that projects out from a sloping roof.

37. The two-pronged end of a hammer used for pulling nails.

38. A rim, collar, or ring on a pipe.

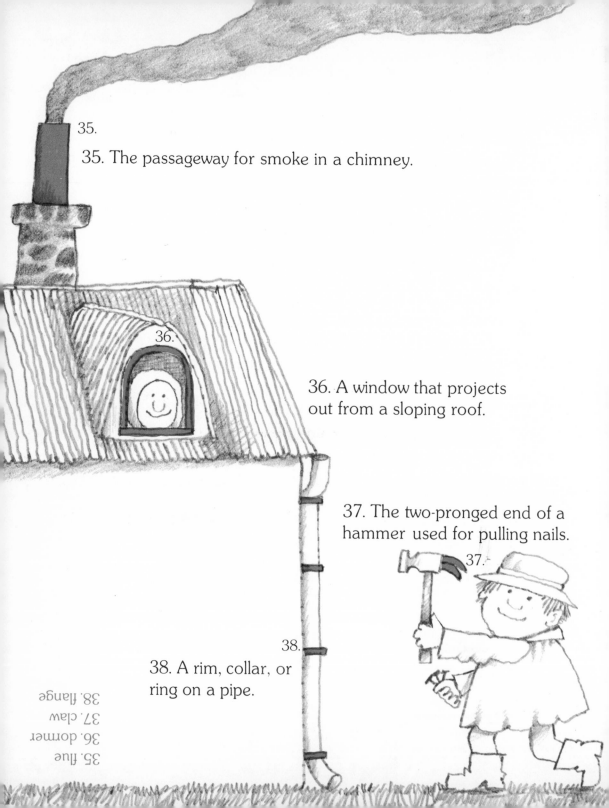

35. flue
36. dormer
37. claw
38. flange

DOOHICKEYS YOU SEE ON PEOPLE OR OTHER ANIMALS

1. The corner at either side of your eye—the place where upper and lower eyelids meet.

2. The flat place at either side of your forehead.

3. Growths of hair down the sides of a man's face just in front of his ears.

TEX STARR

1. canthus
2. temple
3. sideburns

4. A partial wig or hairpiece worn by a man.

5. The bony ridge on top of your nose.

6. Heavy side-whiskers and a mustache worn with a clean-shaven chin.

7. A set of false teeth.

8. A lock of hair that grows
or falls on the forehead.

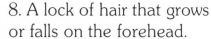

9. The fleshy bump on your
ear between your face and
ear opening.

10. The dividing wall
inside your nose—the
membrane that separates
the two sides.

14. antennae
13. molar
12. uvula
11. canine

11. Any one of your four pointy teeth.

12. The small fleshy piece you can see hanging down in your throat when you stick out your tongue in front of the mirror and say, "Ah."

13. Any one of your flat back teeth.

14. The feelers of insects.

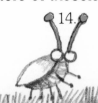

AND
THE COUNT

11.
12.   13.

IN
"3 COWBOYS
MEET
THE VAMPIRE"

15. The bony, branched growths on the heads of male deer-related animals.

15.

16. A claw of a lobster or crab.

16.

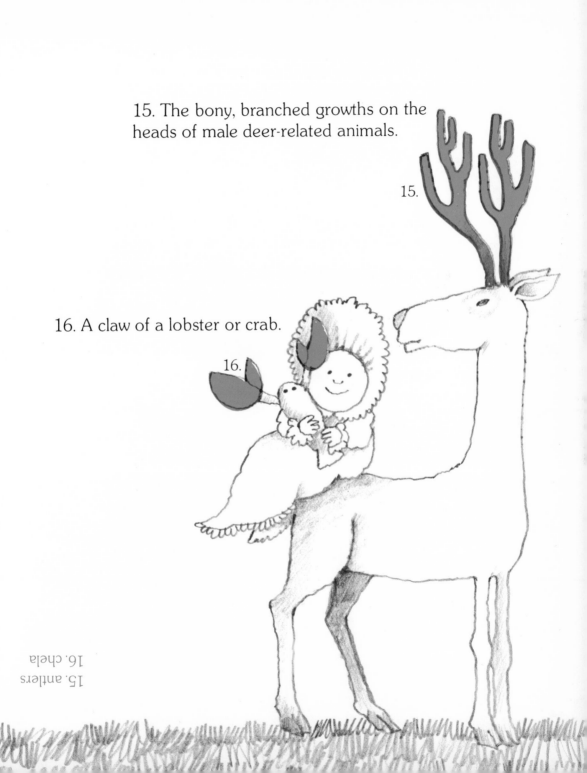

17. A small lump on the skin of
a person or other animal.

18. The back of your neck.

19. The strip of skin at
the base of a fingernail
or toenail.

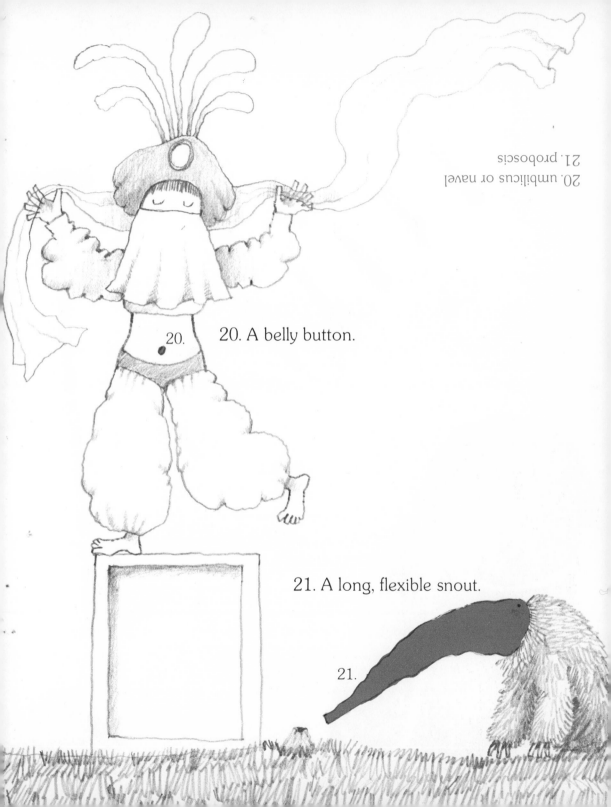

20. umbilicus or navel
21. proboscis

20. A belly button.

21. A long, flexible snout.

WHADYACALLITS YOU MIGHT SEE OUTSIDE

1. A portable trough for carrying bricks or mortar.

2. The rounded bars that are steps on a ladder.

3. Any very big dog.

4. A long, narrow, flat-bottomed sled curved upward and backward in front.

5. rumble seat
6. hip
7. arbor
8. dolly

5. An uncovered passenger seat that sticks out from the rear of an automobile, usually a roadster or a coupe.

6. The orange fruit that appears on a rose bush after the flowering season.

7. A garden shelter made of latticework covered by leafy plants.

8. A handcart with wheels used for moving heavy loads.

9. Any cud-chewing animal.

10. The metal device on a rowboat that holds an oar.

11. A boat race.

12. A young goose.

13. The fruit of an oak tree.

14. A lever for turning the rudder to steer a boat.

15. A long pole that extends from the mast of a boat to hold or extend the foot of a sail.

13.

14.

15.

THINGAMAJIGS THAT HAVE TO DO
WITH WORDS AND NUMBERS

1. A printed page on which many different kinds of type and design are used to attract attention.

2. The small line used to finish off the main stroke on a printed letter.

1.

COMING SOON!

(in 6 pages)
2.

SURPRISES

& 3.

BARGAINS GALORE

at

The Bizarre Bazaar

3. The sign that means "and."

4. The kind of numbers you ordinarily use, as opposed to Roman numerals.

5. A word made from the first letters or groups of letters in a phrase, such as radar from _ra_dio _d_etecting _a_nd _r_anging.

6. In printed matter, three dots (...) to show that something was omitted.

4.
4

5.
RADAR

MARY ●●● 6.
A LITTLE
LAMB

4. Arabic numerals
5. acronym
6. ellipsis

WHATCHAMACALLITS YOU MIGHT SEE ON A TRIP

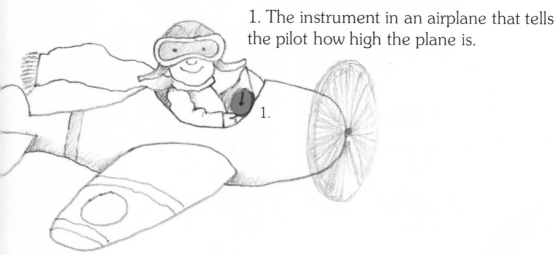

1. The instrument in an airplane that tells the pilot how high the plane is.

1.

1. altimeter 2. plankton

2. The small organisms that drift or float in seawater.

2.

3. A wreath or necklace, usually of flowers or leaves.

4. The basket hanging from the bottom of a balloon to carry passengers or instruments.

5. A sheet of floating ice.

6. A South American fish, not over 1½ feet long, that will attack and eat humans and other large animals.

7. A hat shaped like a flower pot, usually red, and decorated with a long black tassel.

8. A loose, hooded robe worn by North African men.

9. A circus worker who helps put up and take down tents.

10. A seat, often with rails and a canopy, placed on the back of an elephant.

11. A headdress made of a long cloth which is wound or twisted around the head.

12. A large fan that is waved to keep flies from annoying a rajah.

10.

11.

12.

10. howdah 11. turban 12. punkah

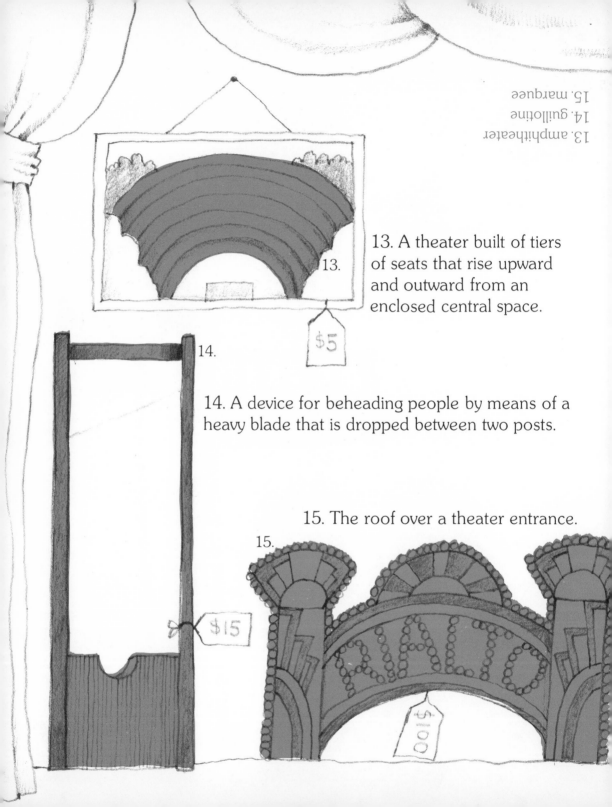

13.

13. A theater built of tiers of seats that rise upward and outward from an enclosed central space.

$5

14.

14. A device for beheading people by means of a heavy blade that is dropped between two posts.

15. The roof over a theater entrance.

15.

$15

RIALTO

$100

16. koala
17. flea market

16.

16. A furry Australian animal that looks like a teddy bear.

17.

17. An open-air market where old or used articles are sold.

$25

$30

WHOSITS YOU MIGHT SEE IF YOU HAPPEN TO BE IN THE RIGHT PLACE AT THE RIGHT TIME

1.

1. The wand used by an orchestra conductor.

2. A person who plays the kettledrums.

3. A small platform for a lecturer, orchestra conductor, etc.

3.

2.

1. baton
2. timpanist
3. podium

4. A group of people hired to applaud at a performance.

5. A kind of firework that makes a loud hissing noise.

6. A short fluffy skirt worn by a ballerina.

4. claque
5. fizgig
6. tutu

7.

7. An eagle's nest, built on a crag
or other high place.

8.

8. The person who takes
care of a church.

9. A portable rock drill that works on compressed air.

9.

10. A special truck for transporting money.

10.

11. The person in charge of keys in a jail.

11.

12. The small grinding device the dentist uses to drill your teeth.

13. The instrument that a doctor plugs into his or her ears to listen to sounds in your chest.

DICAL CENTER

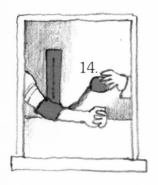

14. The instrument the doctor wraps around your arm to take your blood pressure.

12. burr
13. stethoscope
14. sphygmomanometer

POTS FIXED

15.

15. A person who mends pots or kettles.

16. A frame on the front of a locomotive used to clear the track of obstructions.

16.

17. A large cage or house where birds are kept.

17.

18. A place where bees are kept.

18.

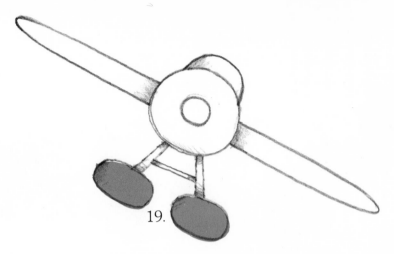

19. The floats that seaplanes have instead of wheels.

A POTPOURRI OF WHOSISES, DINGUSES AND HOWDYACALLITS

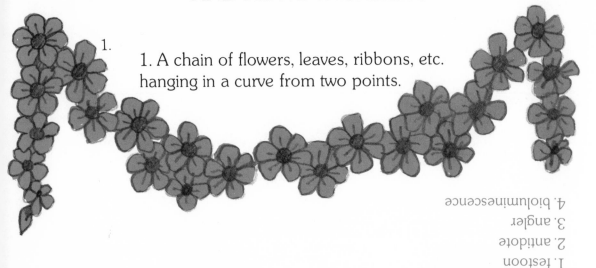

1. A chain of flowers, leaves, ribbons, etc. hanging in a curve from two points.

2. A medicine or other remedy that prevents poison from doing harm.

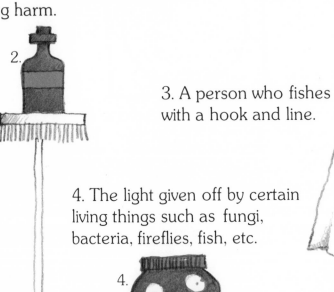

3. A person who fishes with a hook and line.

4. The light given off by certain living things such as fungi, bacteria, fireflies, fish, etc.

5. anemometer
6. afterimage
7. kazoo or mirliton

5.

5. An instrument for measuring wind speed.

6. A thing you can still see after you stop looking at it.

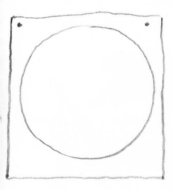

6.

7. A toy musical instrument that consists of a metal tube, open at both ends, with a side hole covered by paper against which the performer sings or hums.

7.

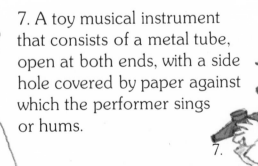

8. A sign with a pointing hand.

9. An obviously fake beard worn by an actor.

10. An object worn by superstitious people to protect them from evil.

11. A female graduate of a particular school, college, or university.

12. A small magnifying glass that a jeweler or watchmaker fits into his eye socket.

13. A drinking mug in the form of a chubby old man wearing a three-cornered hat.

BERNICE KOHN HUNT lives with her husband, author Morton Hunt, in East Hampton, New York. Ms. Hunt studied creative writing at the University of Wisconsin and has been a children's book editor for a leading publishing house. She is actively involved with all the natural life around her home and is an avid organic gardener and cook. She has close to fifty books to her credit, including *The Beachcomber's Book* and the Putnam book *How High is Up?*

TOMIE DE PAOLA studied art at the Pratt Institute and Skowhegan School of Painting and received a Master of Fine Arts from the California College of Arts and Crafts. He has been awarded the Silver Award in the Franklin Prize Competition and has been commended by the American Institute of Graphic Arts.

For Putnam's Tomie has illustrated *Monsters of the Middle Ages, Mario's Mystery Machine*, and *The Mixed-Up Mystery Smell*. He has written and illustrated *Nana Upstairs and Nana Downstairs* and the recent Caldecott Honor Book *Strega Nona*.